Think On These Things for Women

Quotes bible verses, and Affirmations for women

feliciacauley@ymail.com.

www.rightsidepiblishing.com

ISBN- 978-1-955050-09-8

LCCN- 2022922135

Published by Right Side Publishing

Print in the United States

Project manager Robert Cauley

Editor: Felicia S. Cauley

Cover design by Tiny Rhodes

Interior Design by Felicia S Cauley

This book is Dedicated to

My Daughters Micleicia, Johnesha, & Antalicia

Daughters in Christ

Rebecca Salinas

Cassandra Dow

&

my sisters in Christ

Ebonie Banks

Constance Muse

&

Kassandra Mitchell

Think On These Things for Women

Quotes bible verses, and Affirmations for women

Felice S.C

Table Of Contents

YOU ARE A WOMAN WHO IS VERY LOVED BY JESUS CHRIST

"The disciple Jesus loved was sitting next to Jesus at the table."
John 13:23 NLT

CHRIST IS IN YOUR HEART

Christ lives in your heart, and he will help you be the best mother, daughter, or sister you can be. One who is motivated, grounded, and rooted in love.

Ephesians 3:17 That Christ may dwell in your hearts by faith; that ye, being rooted and grounded in love.

GOD'S HEARTBEAT

You are God's heartbeat; he simply adores you. He loved you so much that he sent his son to die for your sins.

1 John 4:10 Herein is love, not that we loved God, but that he loved us, and sent his Son to be the propitiation for our sins.

THINKING GOOD THOUGHTS

We can often fall prey to negative thought patterns which lead to negative feelings. We should always bring our minds back and focus on the right things.

Philippians 4:8 Finally, brethren, whatsoever things are true, whatsoever things are honest, whatsoever things are just, whatsoever things are pure, whatsoever things are lovely, whatsoever things are of good report; if there be any virtue, and if there be any praise, think on these thing

THINK, TALK, WALK, ACT LIKE JESUS

"Therefore become imitators of God [copy Him and follow His example], as well-beloved children [imitate their father];
-1 corinthians 2:16 AMP)

***

THERE IS NOTHING IN THIS WORLD THAT WILL BE IMPOSSIBLE FOR YOU TO DO

"I can do all things [which He has called me to do] through Him who strengthens and empowers me [to fulfill His purpose—I am self-sufficient in Christ's sufficiency; I am ready for anything and equal to anything through Him who infuses me with inner strength and confident peace."- Philippians 4:13 AMP)

YOU CANNOT BE THE SAME WOMAN YOU USED TO BE

"This means that anyone who belongs to Christ has become a new person. The old life is gone; a new life has begun! - 2 Corinthians 5:17 NLT)

***

DON'T BLOCK YOUR BLESSINGS BY LOOKING BACK IN THE PAST

"But Lot's wife, from behind him, [foolishly, longingly] looked [back toward Sodom in an act of disobedience], and she became a pillar of salt.-Genesis 19:26 AMP)

GOD DOES NOT SEE YOUR FLAWS, HE MADE YOU PERFECT JUST THE WAY HE WANTED

"I praise you because I am fearfully and wonderfully made; your works are wonderful, I know that full well".-Psalm 139:14 NIV)

***

Felice S.C

NO ONE HAS THE RIGHT TO JUDGE YOU FOR WHAT YOU HAVE DONE IN THE PAST

"So now there is no condemnation for those who belong to Christ Jesus."Romans 8:1 NLT)

PEOPLE MAY LEAVE YOU, BUT GOD WILL NEVER LEAVE YOU

"Who shall separate us from the love of Christ? Shall trouble or hardship or persecution or famine or nakedness or danger or sword?" -Romans 8:35 NIV)

YOU CANNOT PLEASE GOD AND PEOPLE AT THE SAME TIME. CHOSE TO PLEASE GOD, HE IS THE ONE THAT WILL BE ALWAYS BY YOUR SIDE

"Am I now trying to win the approval of human beings, or of God? Or am I trying to please people? If I were still trying to please people, I would not be a servant of Christ". - Galatians 1:10 NIV)

DELIGHT IN THE LORD

If you delight in the Lord, spend time with him, pray, read his word, and simply enjoy his presence. Soon your heart will align with his. You will want the same things he does. And he will give you the desires of your heart.

Psalm 37:4 Take delight in the LORD, and he will give you the desires of your heart.

GOD'S BEAUTIFUL CREATION

God was careful and intentional when he created you. You are more beautiful than you could ever imagine.

Psalm 139:14 I will praise thee; for I am fearfully and wonderfully made: marvellous are thy works; and that my soul knoweth right well.

AN IMAGE OF GOD

You are the only creation of God that was made to be a reflection him. In everything you do, always remember that you are representing God's image and nature.

Genesis 1: 27 So God created man in his own image, in the image of God created he him; male and female created he them

GOD HEARS YOU WHEN YOU CRY

God keeps your tears in a bottle. He cares about you. He hears you when you cry and sees everything you are going through.

Psalms 56: 8 Thou tellest my wanderings: put thou my tears into thy bottle: are they not in thy book?

YOU ARE MORE THAN YOUR ROLES

As women, we have so many titles.
Daughter, Sister, Niece, Mother, and Wife.
Teachers, caretakers, homemakers,
providers. You are much more than those
titles. Your worth is far above what can be
expressed by words.

*Proverbs 31:10 Who can find a virtuous
woman? for her price is far above rubies.*

DO THAT VERY THING GOD HAS PLACED IN YOUR HEART, WITHOUT FEAR

"For God has not given us a spirit of fear and timidity, but of power, love, and self-discipline"-.2 Timothy 1:17 NLT)

***

EVERYTHING YOU DO IN THE WILL OF GOD, WILL SUCCEED

"And we know that in all things God works for the good of those who love him, who have been called according to his purpose". - Romans 8:28 NIV)

***

NOTHING CAN SEPARATE YOU FROM GOD'S LOVE

There is nothing that can ever stop God from loving you and wanting to be in a relationship with you. Through any trials and tears remember that he is with you and he will not leave you.

Romans 8:38-39 For I am persuaded, that neither death, nor life, nor angels, nor principalities, nor powers, nor things present, nor things to come, Nor height, nor depth, nor any other creature, shall be able to separate us from the love of God, which is in Christ Jesus our Lord.

STAND FIRM IN GOD

As long as you hold on to God you will not be moved by any challenges and trials that threaten to overcome you. He will help you.

Psalm 46:5 God is in the midst of her; she shall not be moved: God shall help her, and that right early.

DO NOT BE AFRAID TO MENTION JESUS WHEN YOU ARE AROUND PEOPLE

"If anyone is ashamed of me and my message, the Son of Man will be ashamed of that person when he returns in his glory and in the glory of the Father and the holy angels."-Luke 9:26 NLT)

***

BE THE ONE TELLING PEOPLE ABOUT THE GOOD NEWS OF THE LORD JESUS CHRIST

"And He said unto them, Go ye into all the world, and preach the gospel to every creature". -Mark 16:15 KJV)

***

FEAR OF GOD

The most valuable trait in a woman is fear of the Lord.

Proverbs 31:30 Favour is deceitful, and beauty is vain: but a woman that feareth the LORD, she shall be praised.

GOD'S PLAN FOR YOU.

God has made a special plan for your life. A good plan, exactly the plan you would choose if you knew everything that he knows.

Jeremiah 29:11 For I know the thoughts that I think toward you, saith the LORD, thoughts of peace, and not of evil, to give you an expected end.

LET GOD PLAN YOUR FUTURE, HE KNOWS WHAT YOU NEED.

"For I know the plans I have for you," says the LORD. "They are plans for good and not for disaster, to give you a future and a hope" -. Jeremiah 29:11 NLT)

ALWAYS REJOICE

In everything you do and go through.
Through the good times and bad times,
always rejoice in the lord, because you can
be sure that at any given time, he is doing
what is best for you.

*Philippians 4:4 Rejoice in the Lord alway:
and again I say, Rejoice.*

DAUGHTERS OF THE MOST HIGH

Today and every day, you can walk with confidence in the full knowledge that God is truly your father, and you are his daughter.

2 Corinthians 6:18 And will be a Father unto you, and ye shall be my sons and daughters, saith the Lord Almighty.

BE CAREFUL ABOUT THE THINGS YOU SAY AS A WOMAN OF GOD.

"The tongue can bring death or life; those who love to talk will reap the consequences". Proverbs 18:21 NLT)

DO NOT BE A WOMAN WHO BEHAVES THE SAME WAY AS PEOPLE WHO DO NOT BELIEVE IN GOD

"So this I say, and solemnly affirm together with the Lord [as in His presence], that you must no longer live as the [unbelieving] Gentiles live, in the futility of their minds [and in the foolishness and emptiness of their souls]"-,Ephesians 4:17 AMP)

REPLACE WORRY WITH PEACE

Whenever you feel worried or anxious about anything. Approach God's throne of grace with humility and gratitude and pray. If you do this, God promises to give you peace.

Philippians 4: 6-7 Be careful about nothing; but in everything by prayer and supplication with thanksgiving let your requests be made known unto God. And the peace of God, which passeth all understanding, shall keep your hearts and minds through Christ Jesus.

GOD IS THE ONLY ONE WHO CAN GIVE YOU REAL JOY AND PEACE.

"May the God of hope fill you with all joy and peace in believing, so that by the power of the Holy Spirit you may abound in hope." Romans 15:13 ESV)

NO ROOM FOR FEAR

When you are afraid. Remind yourself that fear does not come from God. What comes from God is power, love, and a sound mind.

2 Timothy 1:7 For God hath not given us the spirit of fear; but of power, and of love, and of a sound mind KJV

GOD DID NOT PLACE FEAR IN YOU WHEN HE MADE YOU

For the Spirit God gave us does not make us timid, but gives us power, love, and self-discipline.- 2 Timothy 1:7 NLT)

DON'T FEAR PEOPLE THAT PLAN TO DO YOU HARM

"The LORD will cause your enemies who rise against you to be defeated before your face; they shall come out against you one way and flee before you seven ways."- Deuteronomy 28:7 NKJV)

GOD HAS THE PERFECT TIMING

God knows exactly what you need and when. Wait on him, and he will renew your strength.

Isaiah 40:31 But they that wait upon the LORD shall renew their strength; they shall mount up with wings as eagles; they shall run, and not be weary; and they shall walk, and not faint.

YOUR LIFE WILL NOT BE CUT SHORT, BECAUSE GOD HAS PROMISED YOU A LONG LIFE

"With long life I will satisfy him and show him my salvation."Psalm 91:16 NIV)

GOD HAS A JOB FOR YOU TO DO FOR HIS KINGDOM

"For we are his workmanship, created in Christ Jesus for good works, which God prepared beforehand, that we should walk in them."
Ephesians 2:10 ESV)

***

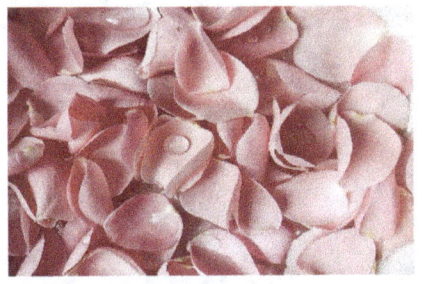

BELIEVE THAT GOD WILL DO WHAT HE SAID IN HIS WORD ABOUT YOU. IT WILL COME TO PASS.

"Faith shows the reality of what we hope for; it is the evidence of things we cannot see".-Hebrews 11:1 NLT)

Felice S.C

GOD IS CAPABLE OF DOING THE IMPOSSIBLE IN YOUR LIFE.

"For with God nothing [is or ever] shall be impossible."
-Luke 1:37 AMP)

NEVER GIVE UP ON THE THINGS YOU HAVE STARTED WORKING ON.

"But you, take courage! Do not let your hands be weak, for your work shall be rewarded." -2 chronicles 15:7 ESV)

***

HOW TO BE SATISFIED

Nothing, not even water in a scorching hot desert, not even bread when you are starving, no man or possession can ever satisfy you like Jesus can.

John 6:35 And Jesus said unto them, I am the bread of life: he that cometh to me shall never hunger; and he that believeth on me shall never thirst.

DONOT DESIRE TO HAVE SOMETHING/ OR SOMEONE THAT BELONGS TO SOMEONE ELSE

"You shall not covet [that is, selfishly desire and attempt to acquire] your neighbor's house; you shall not covet your neighbor's wife, or his male servant, or his female servant, or his ox, or his donkey, or anything that belongs to your neighbor."Exodus 20:17 AMP)

***

CONFIDENCE IN GOD'S WILL

"As long as you are in God's will, everything happening in your life, whether good or bad is working for your good.

Romans 8:28 And we know that all things work together for good to them that love God, to them who are the called according to his purpose.

**MAKE SURE TO PLEASE GOD
IN EVERYTHING YOU DO, SAY,
PLAN, EAT, DRINK, BUY,
WEAR, WATCH, LISTEN TO,
AND WITH THE PEOPLE YOUR
INVOLVE WITH.**

"So whether you eat or drink, or whatever
you do, do it all for the glory of God". -1
Corinthians 10:31 NLT)

***

Felice S.C

PLACE THE WORD IN YOUR HEART, SO THAT IT MAY GO WELL WITH YOU IN LIFE

"Your word is a lamp for my feet, a light on my path". - Psalm 119:105 NIV)

***

YOU DO NOT OWN YOURSELF ANYMORE

"For ye are bought with a price: therefore, glorify God in your body, and in your spirit, which are God's" -.1 corinthians 6:20 KJV

***

Felice S.C

ON INNER BEAUTY

We are so much more than our outward appearance and environment. Our greatest beauty and our greatest value is found in our inner spirit.

2 Corinthians 4: 16 For which cause we faint not; but though our outward man perish, yet the inward man is renewed day by day.

YOU ARE UNIQUE, THERE IS NO ONE LIKE YOU AND THERE WILL NEVER BE ONE, SO NEVER COMPARE YOURSELF TO ANYONE ELSE.

(We do not dare to classify or compare ourselves with some who commend themselves. When they measure themselves by themselves and compare themselves with themselves, they are not wise. 2 Corinthians 10:12 NIV)

GOD WILL FULFILL HIS PROMISES TO YOU.

When you feel your hope or faith shaking or wavering. Remember the character of the one who has made promises to you. He is faithful and never breaks his word.

Hebrews 10:23 Let us hold fast the profession of our faith without wavering; (for he is faithful that promised;)

GOD WILL BRING TO PASS THE THINGS HE HAS PROMISED YOU

"It was by faith that even Sarah was able to have a child, though she was barren and was too old. She believed that God would keep his promise. -Hebrew 11:11 NLT)

Felice S.C

NO NEED FOR SHAME IN GOD'S PRESENCE

Shame cannot stand in the way of God's love for you. God will lift your head.

Psalm 3:3 But thou, O LORD, art a shield for me; my glory, and the lifter up of mine head.

FORGIVE YOURSELF FOR YOUR MISTAKE, GOD WILL NOT REMEMBER THEM.

"He shall again have compassion on us; He will subdue and tread underfoot our wickedness [destroying sin's power]. Yes, You will cast all our sins Into the depths of the sea. Micah 7:19 AMP)

TWO WRONGS DON'T MAKE A RIGHT.

Two wrongs can never make a right. Evil can only be conquered by good.

Romans 12:21, KJV: "Be not overcome of evil, but overcome evil with good.

LIFE IS FULL OF SEASONS.

You were made for such a time as this. Where you are now is exactly where you should be.

Ecclesiastes 3:1 To everything there is a season, and a time to every purpose under the heaven:

KNOW WHEN TO SPEAK, AND KNOW WHEN TO KEEP QUIET.

Wherefore, my beloved brethren, let every man be swift to hear, slow to speak, slow to wrath: James 1:19 KJV

DO NOT LET THE DEVIL USE YOUR MOUTH, TO SPEAK LIES.

"Then keep your tongue from speaking evil and your lips from telling lies". -Psalm 34:13 NLT)

SAY THINGS THAT WILL UPLIFT THE PEOPLE IN YOUR LIFE

"Kind words are like honey— sweet to the soul and healthy for the body. Proverbs 16:24 NLT)

EVERYTHING YOU DO CAN BE WORSHIP.

The worship of God is not confined to prayer and singing only. If in whatever you do, you do it as if you are doing it for God; it becomes an act of worship.

Colossians 3: 23 And whatsoever ye do, do it heartily, as to the Lord, and not unto men

STAY IN GOD'S PRESENCE, AND SEE HOW HE WILL CHANGE YOUR LIFE

"Delight yourself in the LORD, And He will give you the desires and petitions of your heart". -Psalm 37:4 AMP)

***

IF YOU DO THINGS WITHOUT LOVE, THEN IT'S LIKE YOU HAVEN'T DONE ANYTHING

"And if I have prophetic powers, and understand all mysteries and all knowledge, and if I have all faith, so as to remove mountains, but have not love, I am nothing. 1 Corinthians 13:2 NLT)

ACT IN LOVE.

Our actions only have meaning when they are motivated by love.

1 Corinthians 13:1 Though I speak with the tongues of men and of angels, and have not charity, I am become as sounding brass, or a tinkling cymbal.

TRUST IN GOD, EVEN WHEN YOU DON'T UNDERSTAND.

If you are finding it difficult to understand what God is doing. That is okay. You do not have to understand. You only must trust.

Isaiah 55:8-9 my thoughts are not your thoughts, neither are your ways my ways, saith the LORD. For as the heavens are higher than the earth, so are my ways higher than your ways, and my thoughts than your thoughts.

BE CAREFUL WHO YOU PUT YOUR TRUST IN. THE DEVIL USES PEOPLE TO DESTROY OTHERS.

Be sober-minded; be watchful. Your adversary the devil prowls around like a roaring lion, seeking someone to devour. -1 Peter 5:8 ESV

HOW GOD WANTS US TO LIVE

What does God need from us? 'do what is
fair and just, love mercy, and walk humbly.'
A great place to start.

*Micah 6:8 He hath shewed thee, O man,
what is good; and what doth
the LORD require of thee, but to do justly,
and to love mercy, and to walk humbly with
thy God*

STAND ON THE THINGS YOU SAY, DON'T CHANGE YOUR OPINION TO PLEASE SOMEONE ELSE.

"But most of all, my brothers and sisters, never take an oath, by heaven or earth or anything else. Just say a simple yes or no, so that you will not sin and be condemned.-James 5:12 NLT

YOUR WORDS NEEDS TO MATCH YOUR ACTIONS

"These people honor me with their lips, but their hearts are far from me. -Matthew 15:8 NLT)

BE CAREFUL ABOUT THE THINGS YOU SAY AS A WOMAN OF GOD

"The tongue can bring death or life; those who love to talk will reap the consequences". Proverbs 18:21 NLT)

LET GOD BE THE FIRST ONE YOU TALK TO WHEN YOU WAKE UP

"But I, O LORD, cry to you; in the morning my prayer comes before you" -Psalm 88:13 ESV)

ARE YOU GROWING IN CHRIST?

If you want to see if you are growing in Christ, check your fruit. Are you patient? Joyful? Do you have the fruits of the spirit?

Galatians 5:22-23 But the fruit of the Spirit is love, joy, peace, longsuffering, gentleness, goodness, faith, Meekness, temperance: against such there is no law.

STAY AWAY FROM DRAMA IF YOU WANT TO LIVE A PEACEFUL LIFE

"Who is the man who desires life And loves many days, that he may see good? Keep your tongue from evil And your lips from speaking deceit. Psalm 34:12-13 AMP

Felice S.C

ALWAYS STAY CLOSE TO THE LORD JESUS CHRIST

"Abide in me, and I in you. As the branch cannot bear fruit by itself, unless it abides in the vine, neither can you, unless you abide in me."
-John 15:4 ESV)

YOU CANNOT WALK WITH CHRIST AND EXPECT EVERYONE TO LIKE YOU.

"And you will be hated by everyone because of [your association with] My name, but it is the one who has patiently persevered and endured to the end who will be saved. Matthew 10:22 AMP)

***

TRUST IN GOD ALWAYS

Before you do anything, you need to involve God, pray to him for guidance, and acknowledge him because our minds and hearts can deceive us. It is always better to trust in God.

Proverbs 3:5-6 Trust in the LORD with all thine heart; and lean not unto thine own understanding. In all thy ways acknowledge him, and he shall direct thy paths.

ON GENEROSITY

Jesus calls us to be generous just as he is generous. He promises us that if we give, he will meet our every need.

Luke 6:38 "give, and it will be given to you. Good measure, pressed down, shaken together, running over, will be put into your lap. For with the measure you use it will be measured back to you.

NEVER DO THINGS TO BE NOTICED BY PEOPLE

" I do not receive glory from people.-John 5:41 ESV)

YOU CANNOT RECEIVE IF YOU DO NOT GIVE.

Give, and you will receive. Your gift will return to you in full—pressed down, shaken together to make room for more, running over, and poured into your lap. The amount you give will determine the amount you get back." Luke 6:38 NLT

YOU WILL ALWAYS RECEIVE BACK WHAT YOU DO IN LIFE, GOOD OR BAD

"Don't be misled—you cannot mock the justice of God. You will always harvest what you plant. -Galatians 6:7 NLT)

PRAY FOR GOD TO GIVE YOU MULTIPLE STREAMS OF INCOME

"Invest in seven ventures, yes, in eight; you do not know what disaster may come upon the land." -Ecclesiastic 11:2 NIV)

***

EXPECT GOD TO DO NEW THINGS IN YOUR LIFE

(For I am about to do something new. See, I
have already begun! Do you not see it? I
will make a pathway through the wilderness.
I will create rivers in the dry wasteland.
Isaiah 43:19 NLT)

BE A WOMAN WHO PRAYS FOR THOSE WHO CANNOT PRAY FOR THEMSELVES

"I urge you, first of all, to pray for all people. Ask God to help them; intercede on their behalf and give thanks for them.") -1 timothy 2:1 NLT

YOUR PRAYERS WILL NEVER BE IN VAIN

(But when you pray, go away by yourself, shut the door behind you, and pray to your Father in private. Then your Father, who sees everything, will reward you. Matthew 6:6 NLT

ALWAYS PRAY WITHOUT DOUBTING

"Therefore, I tell you, whatever you ask for in prayer, believe that you have received it, and it will be yours"-. Mark 11:24 NIV)

BELIEVE THAT GOD WILL DO WHAT HE SAID IN HIS WORD ABOUT YOU. IT WILL COME TO PASS

"Faith shows the reality of what we hope for; it is the evidence of things we cannot see". -Hebrews 11:1 NLT)

GOD WILL RESCUE YOU

If you find yourself trapped or lost in your life. God says that he will rescue you.

Ezekiel 34:11-12 For thus saith the Lord GOD; Behold, I, even I, will both search my sheep, and seek them out. As a shepherd seeketh out his flock in the day that he is among his sheep that are scattered; so will I seek out my sheep, and will deliver them out of all places where they have been scattered in the cloudy and dark day.

FILL YOUR SPIRIT MAN WITH THE THINGS OF GOD, SO THAT DEMONS MAY NOT HAVE ANY LEGAL RIGHT IN YOUR LIFE

"Then it says, 'I will return to the person I came from. 'So, it returns and finds its former home empty, swept, and in order. Then it goes and takes with it seven other spirits more wicked than itself, and they go in and live there. And the final condition of that person is worse than the first. That is how it will be with this wicked generation." Matthew 12:44-45 NIV

***

GOD HAS GIVEN YOU THE AUTHORITY TO BREAK CURSES IN YOUR LIFE

"And your ancient ruins shall be rebuilt; you shall raise up the foundations of many generations; you shall be called the repairer of the breach, the restorer of streets to dwell in. Isaiah 58:12 ESV)

YOU CANNOT TAKE EVERYONE WITH YOU ON THE JOURNEY GOD IS TAKING YOU ON

"Is not the entire land before you? Please separate [yourself] from me. If you take the left, then I will go to the right; or if you choose the right, then I will go to the left." -Genesis 13:9 AMP)

DON'T BE FRIENDS WITH PEOPLE WHO DON'T LIKE THE GOD YOU SERVE

"Blessed is the one who does not walk in step with the wicked or stand in the way that sinners take or sit in the company of mockers, Psalm 1:1 NIV)

***

IT'S BETTER TO HAVE ONE LOYAL FRIEND BY YOUR SIDE, THEN TO HAVE TEN FAKE ENVIOUS FRIENDS

"Faithful are the wounds of a friend [who corrects out of love and concern], But the kisses of an enemy are deceitful [because they serve his hidden agenda]. -Proverbs 27:6 AMP

GOD IS OUR STRENGTH.

You may be weak in every way possible, but you will persevere because the everlasting God is the source of your strength.

Psalms 73:26 My flesh and my heart faileth: but God is the strength of my heart, and my portion for ever.

HOW TO TREAT YOUR NEIGHBOR

Always remember to treat others as you would like to be treated.

Luke 6:31 And as ye would that men should do to you, do ye also to them likewise.

GOD IS ALWAYS THINKING OF YOU.

God sees you and he thinks of you all the time. He loves you deeply.

Psalm 139:17-18 How precious also are thy thoughts unto me, O God! how great is the sum of them! If I should count them, they are more in number than the sand: when I awake, I am still with thee.

DON'T TURN YOUR HEART AWAY FROM GOD BY BEING WITH SOMEONE WHO IS NOT SENT BY HIM

"As Solomon grew old, his wives turned his heart after other gods, and his heart was not fully devoted to the LORD his God, as the heart of David his father had been. - 1 Kings 11:4 NIV

THE LORD IS WATCHING YOUR EVERY STEP

"The LORD is watching everywhere, keeping his eye on both the evil and the good. -Proverbs 15:3 NLT)

ASK GOD FOR WISDOM TO MAKE THE RIGHT DECISIONS IN LIFE.

"For the LORD gives [skillful and godly] wisdom; From His mouth come knowledge and understanding." -Proverbs 2:6 AMP)

GOD WILL GIVE YOU HIS FAVOR WHENEVER YOU NEED IT.

"But Noah found favor and grace in the eyes of the LORD"-. Genesis 6:8 AMP)

***

DO WHAT GOD HAS TOLD YOU TO DO, AND THINGS WILL WORK OUT WELL IN YOUR LIFE.

("My child, never forget the things I have taught you. Store my commands in your heart."-Proverbs 3:)

***

THERE IS NO DISEASE IN THIS WORLD THAT GOD CANNOT HEAL, ASK GOD FOR HEALING IN FAITH AND HE WILL HEAL YOU.

("Let all that I am praise the LORD; may I never forget the good things he does for me. He forgives all my sins and heals all my diseases."- Psalm 103:2-3 NLT)

DO NOT RUIN THIS DAY BY WORRYING ABOUT ANOTHER DAY

"Therefore, do not worry about tomorrow, for tomorrow will worry about itself. Each day has enough trouble of its own".
Matthew 6:34 NIV)

**

IT WILL BE HARD FOR YOU TO SIN IF YOU READ HIS WORD AND SPEND TIME EVERY DAY WITH GOD

"So I say, walk by the Spirit, and you will not gratify the desires of the flesh".- Galatians 5:16 NIV)

***

DON'T LET UNFORGIVENESS TAKE ROOT IN YOUR HEART, IT WILL HINDER YOUR PRAYERS.

("For if you forgive others their trespasses [their reckless and willful sins], your heavenly Father will also forgive you".- Matthew 6:14 AMP)

***

NEVER HURT SOMEONE WHO HAS HURT YOU, PUT IT IN GOD'S HANDS. THE GOD WHO MADE THE EYES, SEES EVERYTHING

"Dear friends, never take revenge. Leave that to the righteous anger of God. For the Scriptures say, "I will take revenge; I will pay them back," says the LORD."- Romans 12:19 NLT)

***

CHOSEN BY CHRIST.

Despite what you may think, you never chose Jesus. Jesus chose you. That is how special you are to him.

John 15:16 Ye have not chosen me, but I have chosen you, and ordained you, that ye should go and bring forth fruit, and that your fruit should remain: that whatsoever ye shall ask of the Father in my name, he may give it you.

DARE TO TALK ABOUT JESUS, WHEREVER YOU GO.

("If anyone is ashamed of me and my message, the Son of Man will be ashamed of that person when he returns in his glory and in the glory of the Father and the holy angels.")
-Luke 9:26 NLT

THE WOMAN YOU WERE CREATED TO BE.

God has created you to be a strong and honourable woman. One who is wise and kind.

Proverbs 31:25 Strength and honour are her clothing; and she shall rejoice in time to come. She openeth her mouth with wisdom; and in her tongue is the law of kindness.

DO NOT ACCEPT THE WRONG PACKAGE

You deserve to have what GOD Has For you Do not settle for less, God's way is the best way.

" I appeal to you, brothers, to watch out for those who cause divisions and create obstacles contrary to the doctrine that you have been taught; avoid them. For such persons do not serve our Lord Christ, but their own appetites, and by smooth talk and flattery they deceive the hearts of the naive. Romans 16:17-18 ESV

AMAZING GRACE

This is the gospel. This is amazing grace. That Jesus loved you so much that he gave up his own life. So never believe that you are unloved, or worthless. You are worth the blood of Jesus.

John 15:13 Greater love hath no man than this, that a man lay down his life for his friends.

If this book has blessed you, please take the time to write a review on Amazon and Barnes and Noble, or wherever you have purchased this book. Share this book with your friends, prayer groups, churches, and on all platforms to build and strengthen women. Thank you, for your support! We would love to hear from you, email us at rightsideceo@yahoo.com for publishing visit the website below
www.rightsidepublishing.com